'SURGE'

I0472288

THE FILM SCRIPT

**A film written and directed by Her Holiness
Gabriel A. Thirteen**

From the novel by **Jonathan R P Taylor**

'MEAT - Memoirs of A Psychopath. The Definitive Edition 2023'

Available from: https://www.lulu.com/spotlight/brittunculi

Starring:

'The Brotherhood and Their Victims'

With a rather thin performance by **Isabella Davies**

And special bit part by dear **Brian Wilkinson C.B.E**

Location: Buzludzha Communist House, Bulgaria

Genre: Classical Horror / Supernatural

We are aware that a number of re-enactment and parody versions of 'Surge' have been recreated by over-enthusiastic amateur filmmakers, fans and readers alike. Because of such events, by statute law the Bulgarian authorities have instructed that the site, Buzludzha, be permanently sealed. **Trespasses now face immediate arrest and imprisonment.** Whilst re-enactment and parody versions are lawful, in the interests of public safety, we must ask that this practice cease forthwith. If you have made such a film, we would be delighted to receive a copy to share on social media. Anonymous submissions are most welcomed.

Thank you! - Then let us begin...

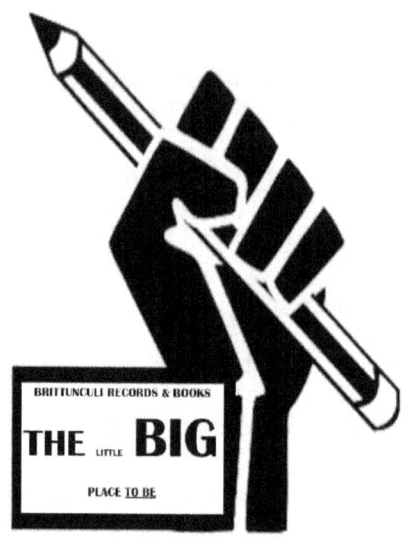

Print, Audio and eBook License Notes

LULU PUBLISHING – FRANCE

ISBN: 978-1-304-80864-6

Imprint: Lulu.com

On screen: Definition appears...

SURGE - *''A sudden powerful forward or upward movement, especially by a crowd or by a natural force such as water or electricity.''*

Additional text now scrolls upward on continued black screen

"It is the summer of 2015. What you are about to see is lost footage now recovered. A horrific catalogue of murder, all captured on DVD, and addressed in person to the UK publishing house; Brittunculi. It was noted FOA: Odd Jonathan. Its delivery was intercepted by covert agents of ARAT. The investigation continues."

OPENING SCENE

A basement unknown. The body of an elderly man is seen to be carved up. Piece by piece his flesh is sliced away and removed by a hooded male. In the background, a young fragile woman is seen. She is chained, hog-tied on a stone slab and clearly weak from starvation. The same hooded figure is seen to feed her, orally, with the human flesh.

The camera now focuses on a message, written in blood along a dank concrete wall. It simply reads 'This is Part Four'.

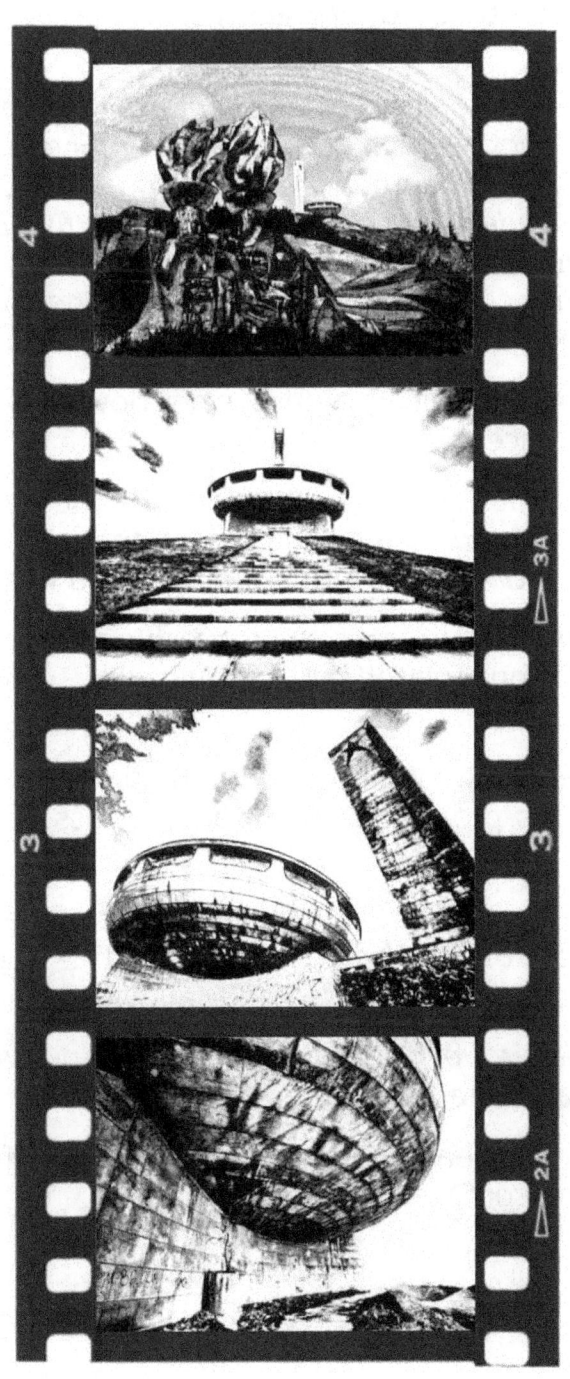

SCENE ONE: Backpacking

Home movie footage of a recent holiday undertaken by a group of six backpackers now takes over. Five of the group are British, the sixth member is a Kiwi from New Zealand and is the group's leader. The camera focuses on five people walking in line ahead of a camera operator who appears to be female judging by her clothes. They are approaching a cylindrical UFO object, atop of a remote secluded hill, in the distance.

Jade: *(Shouts)* Will you guys slow down? I can't film and walk at this pace.

Gunner: *(Replies as walk leader ahead)* You wanted to do the filming today. Anyway a bit of camera shake will all add to the impact won't it? You were the one that said keep it authentic.

Candy: *(Mid group and now laughing)* No pain no gain sweetheart. You wanted to do Bulgaria. I did suggest the Pyrenees this year.

Jade: There's authentic and crap you know. We need this stuff for our Major's project. We do want to pass it after all, fuck-heads.

Kate: *(Nearest to camera turns around to face Jade)* It's not far now. Look, Buzludzha. There she is. This is what we came for. Don't worry about it. We can't fail with a shot like that.

James: *(Mid group interrupts her)* You can always fuck your way to a grade one later Jade, ask Candy!

Candy: You can really be a piece of shit sometimes. I started fucking Professor Dean long after I had finished his module. You fucking know that jerk-off. I wish I'd never told you.

Jade: Children, stop fighting!

Alex: (*Remaining group member*) Yeah, come on dudes. Were here to enjoy ourselves. You know how busy we'll be when we get back. Fuck talking about campus, we deserve a holiday!

Gunner: We need to crack-on. Look. There's a storm coming in, fast. We need to get in there before dark. You don't want to be struck by lightning at this altitude.

James: Fuck aye. Bring it on God!

The group finally arrive, exhausted.

SKETCH: One of nine to follow

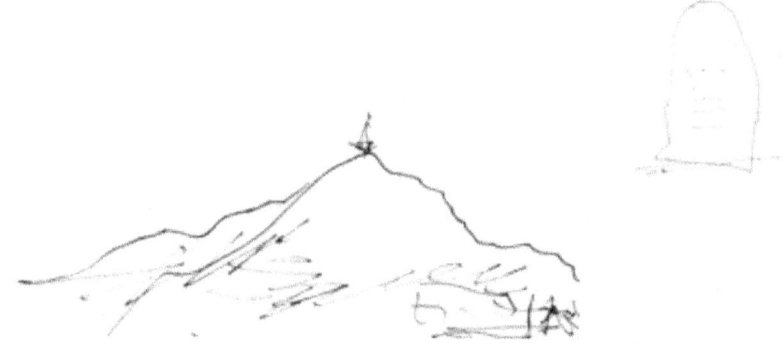

Rare and original. The priceless pen and ink doodles of Buzludzha House architect and designer Georgi Stoilov. Shared with Odd Jonathan during his meeting in March 2015 (Sofia). Reproduced here by kind permission of the Buzludzha Foundation and Her Holiness Gabriela 13.

Georgi Stoilov was born April 3rd, 1929, in Bulgaria. He is one of the founders of the Union of Architects in Bulgaria, the founder of the International Academy for Architecture, and also President of the Union Internationale des Architectes (International Unions of Architects), a position he has held since 1987. His notable world famous works include the monument at Buzludzha, the inverted pyramid building of the Bulgarian Natiional Radio in Sofia, the Freedom Arch at Beklemeto and the Art Gallery of the Union of Bulgarian Artists. He is a former Mayor of the nation's capital, Sofia.

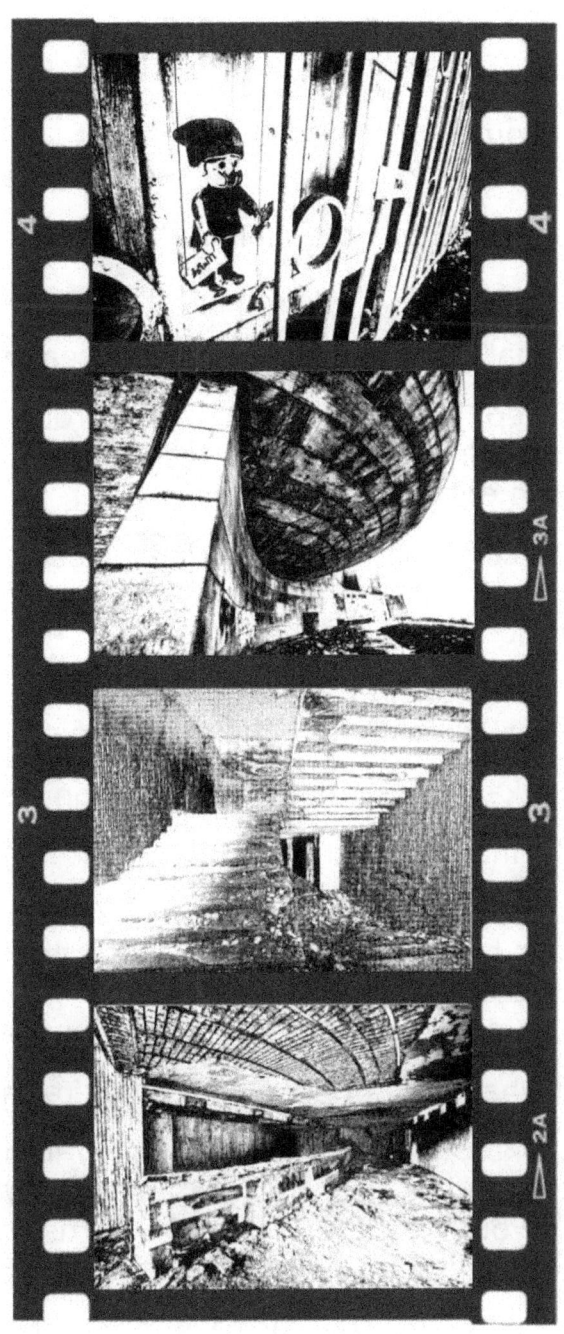

SCENE TWO: *Arrangements*

Jade: (*Group now sitting on steps of Buzludzha main entrance*) I'm fucked, have you seen the state of my feet?

Alex: Me too. What's the plan?

Gunner: Safety, that's what's first! Helmets on!

James: What - are you serious? I'm sweating my bollocks off.

Gunner: Yep. You all appointed me group leader so live with it. No helmets means no insurance cover. It's in the risk assessment, you know that!

Kate: And cameras on at all times please guys. We need to get everything; and seeing as the cameras are helmet mounted, no helmet means no footage.

Alex: We'd better get everything. I'm not doing that trek again, never! I reckon my ankles are going to explode.

Gunner: Okay, have I got your attention now?

Candy: Well get on with it then

Gunner: We have enough battery for all six cameras for twenty-four hours max. That's it. Then we have a choice. Return to the hostel and recharge or get the job done quickly, like now. That means no rest for the wicked!

Kate: So what's the brief? Gunner, you're the team leader.

Gunner: Okay. Here it is then. We stay in pairs for safety reasons. Seeing as (*pointing to Candy and James huddled together*) you two are now love birds, you take the basements together.

James: That's fine by me. Yet another big dark hole to explore.

Candy: (*Giggles*) I hope we'll take our time then. I do like the damp beneath me.

Alex: That's sick you two. Get a room will you!

Gunner: Alex and Jade, you're the experienced climbers, take the tower please.

Jade: Will do!

Gunner: Kate, we'll take the dome.

Kate: Boring!

Gunner: Thought you'd say that, (*Then whispers in her ear*) that's why we do the tunnel first!

Kate: (*Whispers back*) Now you're talking.

Candy: I'm starving to death. I take it we eat now?

Alex: Yeah. Let's eat now before dark, here. The view's amazing. Might as well catch as much of it as we can before sunset.

All: Agreed!

Group unpack camping stoves and prepare dinner on steps as Jade films them.

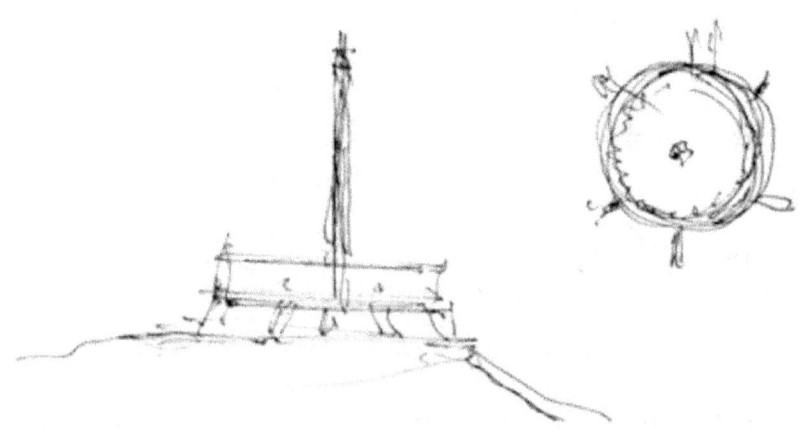

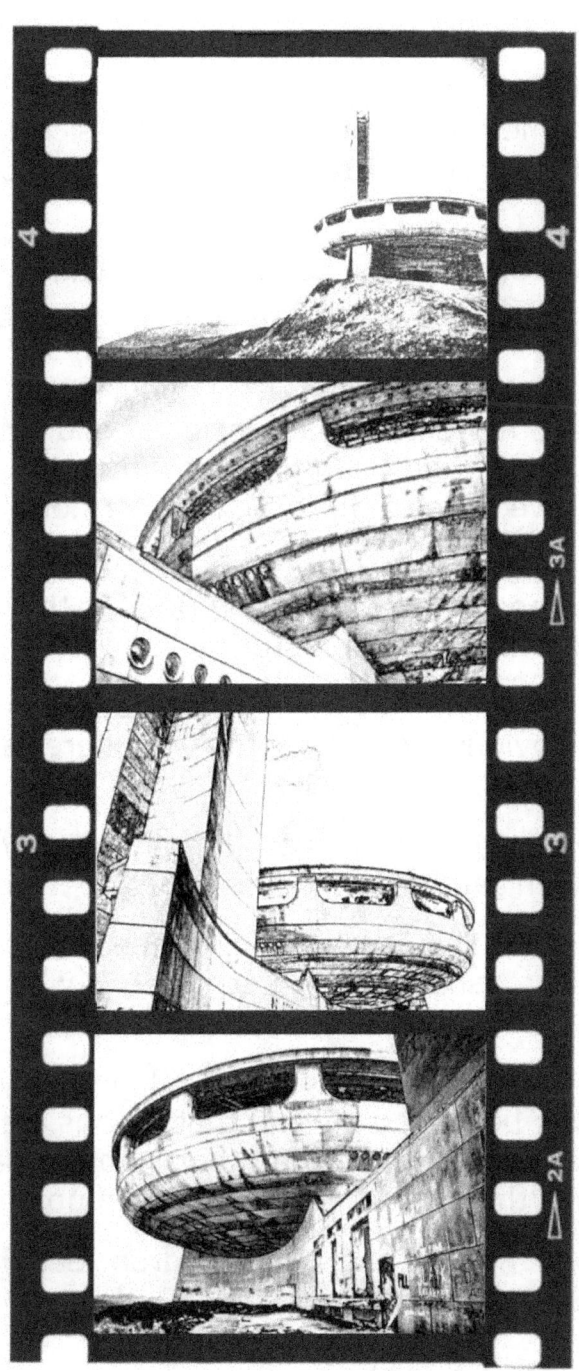

SCENE THREE: *Business*

13

Gunner: Right then, let's pack up and get off. We meet back under the dome, below the hammer and sickle, in six hours. Let's synchronize our watches, mine says it's now just after 6 pm.

Alex: Synchronize to "it's just after 6..." What the fuck?

Kate: Don't be a twat Alex. We're not invading Iraq you know.

Gunner: For fuck's sake then. Its 4 minutes past. Do you need the seconds too? We meet back inside at midnight. If for some reason you can't, then 6 am tomorrow morning is an absolute must, okay! We all leave here together or not at all.

Jade: Leave a note guys. I mean if you get there early there's no point in standing about wasting time, is there Gunner? We can all get on with the other stuff.

Gunner: Good point. But weight the paper down so it doesn't blow away. Obvious I know, but the wind here can be extreme, look at what's left of the roof.

Candy: Can I write mine now then? (*Laughing*). Having a great time with James downstairs. See you in the morning!

Jade: Come on. This is serious. We need to know we are all safe and that means knowing each other's whereabouts at all times.

Gunner: Absolutely. We need to log everything or the University will be pissed off and that means we fail guys! We got our grants for a reason and that involves backing this up with evidence that we did what we signed up and agreed too.

James: Rodger, over and out squadron leader. Catch up at midnight guys, we're off.

Candy: Have fun all, see ya.

Jade: Let's do it then Alex. It's pitch black inside until we get to the top of the tower. I'd like to be there, on top, for sun set.

Alex: Self and torch on its way. You sort the ropes.

Only Gunner and Kate remain.

Gunner: Let's make our move too. We've got a big job on finding that shaft.

Kate: Shaft? I thought we were doing a tunnel.

Gunner: Semantics, semantics. It is a tunnel but almost vertical in places, especially when it breaks out into the lab.

Kate: What fucking lab?

Gunner: You're gonna love it! Mum's the word.

Kate: Stop right there. No secrets, what fuckin' lab?

Gunner: Well, I didn't want to say anything until the others were out of ear shot. Apparently, well according to that drunk Russian we met last night, remember, the one that couldn't keep his eyes of Candy's tits, well, anyway, he said there's a secret military access tunnel that leads into a bunker below the cellars. It was sealed off years ago.

Kate: Why haven't you said anything until now?

Gunner: Because the early bird gets the worm, stupid. And so what? If I had the others would have wanted to come with us and then nothing that we really need to do here today would get finished. Face it Kate. James and Candy would just shag all day and Alex and Jade would just moan about their feet! Anyway, what's the point in us all going if we don't even know if it's true or not.

Kate: And the rest? You're holding back again, I can tell.

Gunner: Wait and see will you.

Kate: No! All of it now! Spill the beans..

Gunner: Don't be such a kill joy, mate. Where's that sense of adventure gone girl?

Kate: (*Prompts Gunner demandingly*) Gunner?

Gunner: For fuck's sake, we're wasting time now. Okay. Laboratory six levels beneath, sealed up after a serious of murders. Is that enough for you?

Oh, I almost forgot. He mentioned countless disappearances too.

Kate: You prick.

Gunner: I know, but don't say it too loudly, I don't have planning permission. Anyway, it's probably all balls, but I just wanna find out either way. But if it's true, think of the grade we're gonna get for finding it. A plus all round.

Kate: Of course it not true. Urbexers would never keep that one down, and seeing as they gave us most of the research data for this trip in the first place, shit for brains, I think somebody would have let that cat out of the bag soon enough, wouldn't they?

Gunner: Urbexers yes, but...

Kate: But what?

Gunner: But what if it wasn't urbexers who said it. What if, just what if it was a certain drunk Russian man who had shown me a video of the entrance? The very same drunken Russian who has now lost his cell phone?

Kate: You didn't? What the fuck Gunner!

Gunner: He doesn't know a thing, trust me. He was way too smashed to remember anything. Look... (*Gunner now shows Kate a phone video of entrance and entry route*). It's easy! Nice phone too!

Kate: We don't know what's in there. It may be unsafe,

snakes, spiders, bears for Christ sake, and anything could go wrong.

Gunner: Look Kate, the decision's yours. You can come with me or be the killjoy and stay here. The Russian said nobody's been up it in years. It's just a service tunnel; an exit route in case of emergency.
But if it does open up into an old laboratory, I want to be the first in. Got it?

Kate: (*Angrily addresses Gunner*) If something goes wrong you'll fuck this trip up for all of us. So here it is. I'll be the adult here if you don't mind, cretin. I'm going inside to do the dome. You can go off and get lost in a shitty make-believe hole if you want to. You're on your own with that one pal. You fuckin' explain yourself to the others, don't involve me!

Gunner: Snooze you lose, girl. Your choice. Helmet, camera, lamps and ropes, nothing can go wrong. So I guess I'll see ya later then?

Gunner disappears into woodland in the far distance whilst Kate watches on angry and bemused. The storm starts to close in with loud cracks of thunder heard overhead. The sky darkens. Her head cam is still filming, both video and audio. Gunner too is filming his walk away as he sings to himself. Kate walks around to the right-hand-side of the building and enters through a hole smashed in the concrete. Steel bars welded together block the original main entrance.

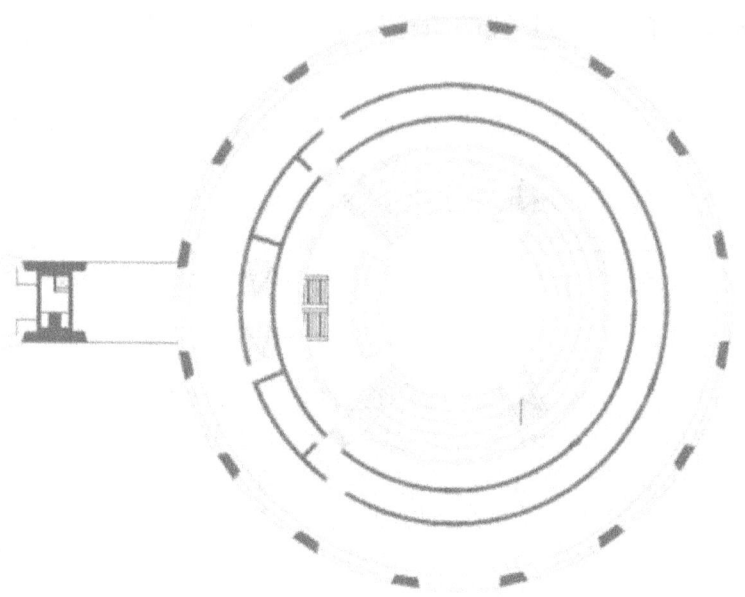

Dome

Georgi Stoilov, original Architect Plan - Main Entrance.

Courtesy of Dora Ivanova: Buzludzha Foundation.

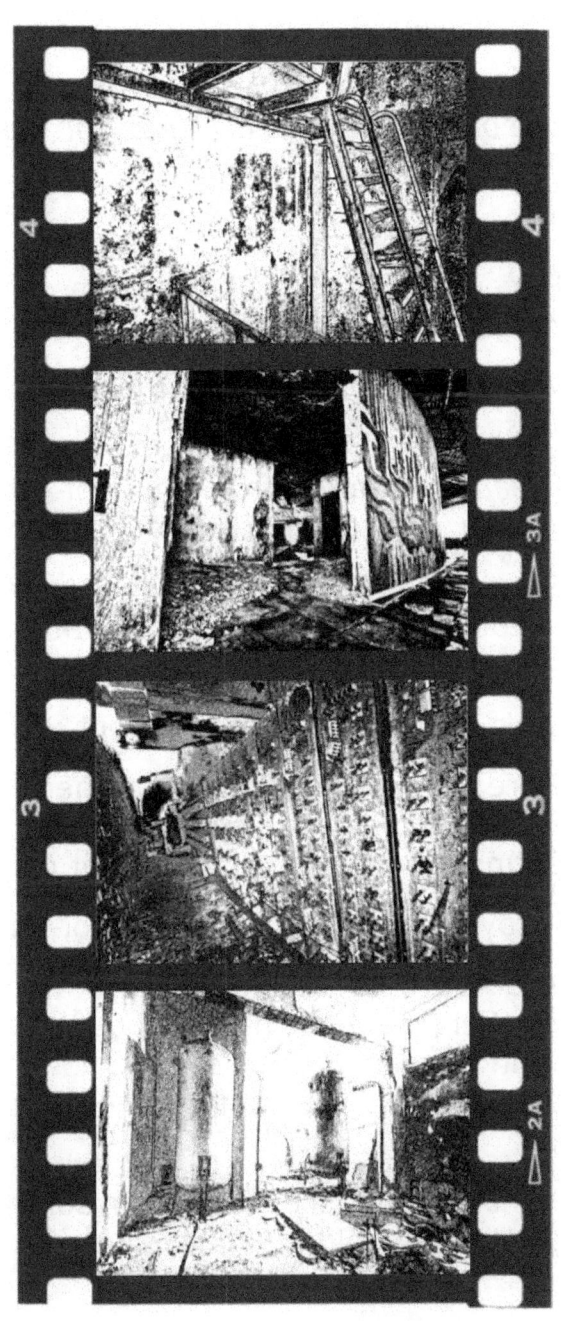

SCENE FOUR: *Basement*

James and Candy film as they both walk down a stairway towards the basement levels. They come across a floral tribute midway in the stairwell.

Candy: What the crap's that for?

James: Haven't got a clue, but it seems to be a memorial to two French guys. Look, there, at the photo.

> *...Camera sees framed text amongst tributes left by others.*

James: (*Reads out aloud*) In memory of Achille Pinet, 23, and Marrok Brideau, 29. Look here? It says murdered on this date.

Candy: So whose great idea was it to upgrade their 3G then? Candy's of course – go girl or what! (*Smug mocking laughter*) I guess you call that girl power?

James: Let's see what you can find out.

Candy: Here; there's a blog about them. It's from a book called 'Meat: Memoirs of a Psychopath'. Scrolling down now...
James: Sounds pretty sick to me. What does it say?

Candy: It says it's a hoax. Some kind of promo thing.

James: Are you sure? Look. Those flowers are rotten, and those ones there next to them are quite recent. And there's everything in between. There's a memorial book, see, under those bottles. It looks like people have been leaving stuff here for years.

Candy: Perhaps we should leave them some wet panties then! Come on, let's keep going. I'll make sure it's worth your while.

James's camera shot catches her tuning back as she walks on blowing him a kiss. She turns away and pats her own arse beckoning him on sexually.

James reads the memorial book and examines other memorial items at the site for a few minutes more whilst left alone. Sprayed on the wall Hashtag Gabrielites. Then continues his journey further downward into the basement to catch up with Candy.

James: (*Shouts*) Candy, Candy! Wait up. (*There is no reply*).

James: Candy! Where are you? This is freaking me out. (*He continues to search for her in the darkness until eventually she jumps out on him*).

Candy: Boo! (*Now laughing*).

James: You fucking bitch! What did you do that for?

Candy: I hear that fear can make a man hard - big boy!

    Candy seductively falls to her knees down toward James's crotch. Head cameras continue to film each other active in passionate sexual scene. Both release loud groans of pleasure as the noise of their sexual coupling echoes out into the darkness.

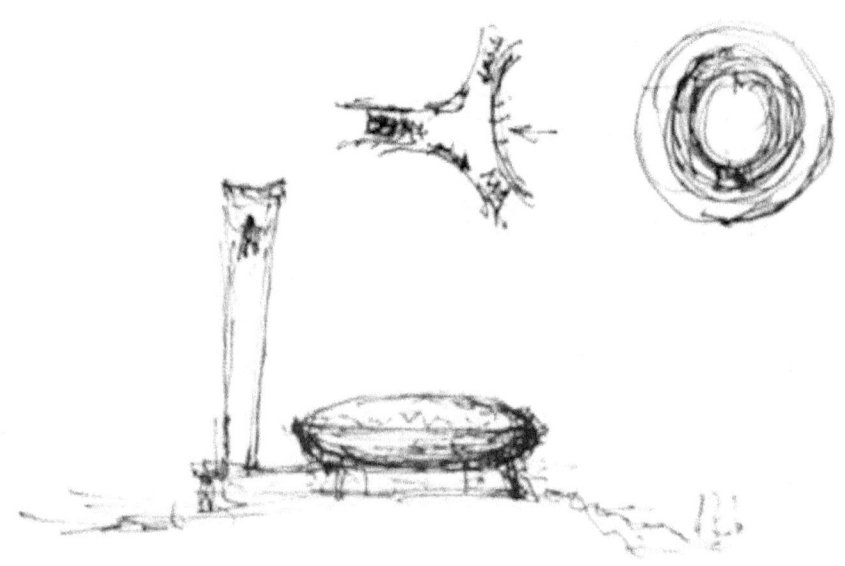

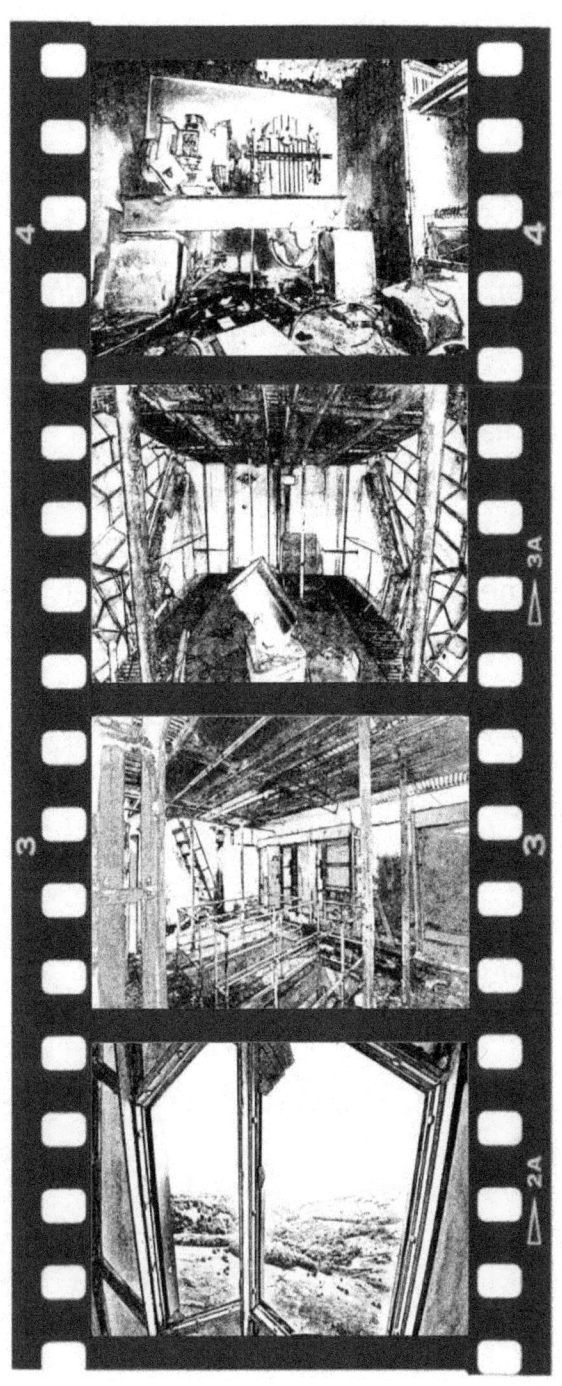

23

SCENE FIVE: Tower

Head cams capture ascent eventually opening up into star room.

Jade: (*First to arrive at the top*) Fuck me; that was some climb but this makes it all worth it. Wait 'til you see this.

Alex: My fucking ankles are killing again. It'd better be good!

Jade: Let me get the script out. You set the tripod up. We need to do the project intro here, and no camera shake this time.

Alex: Jade, you're such a slave driver. Let me know when you've finished rehearsing first. I need at least 10 minutes off my feet. Until then, fuck it all.

Jade: Lightweight!

As Alex rests, pouring a coffee from his flask and lighting a cigarette, Jade practices her narration for the project script.

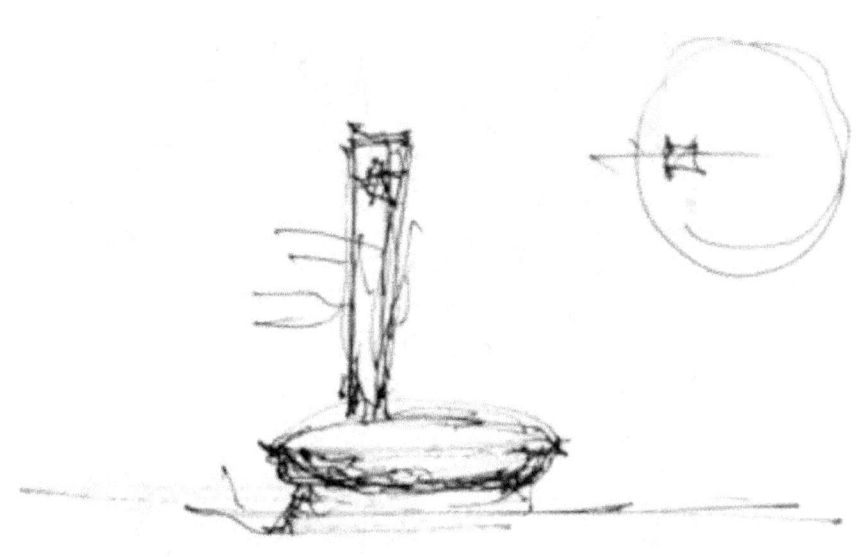

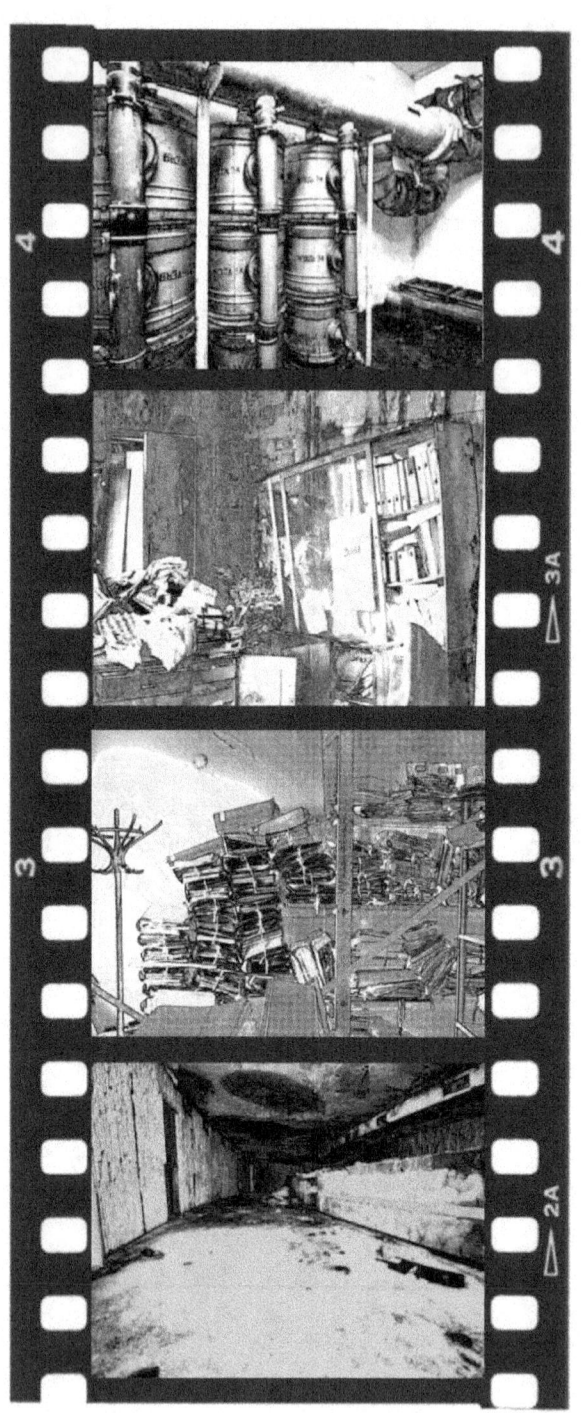

26

SCENE SIX: Ghost

Footage cuts back to scene of intense sexual excitement between Candy and James in basement until Candy suddenly freezes, still as stone.

Candy: What the fuck was that?

James: That's the sound of hard fucking! (*Continuing to thrust into her from her behind*)

Candy: James, seriously, fucking stop already, there's someone down here with us. (*As James ejaculates with loud release*).

James: I hope they enjoyed the show then.

Candy hurriedly tucks her breasts back into her bra and pulls up her jeans.

James: What the fuck, Candy? What's going on? You look like you've just seen a ghost.

Candy: I'm telling you James, there's someone in here with us, my head torch caught them watching us, just a glimpse in the dark, down there, listen.

James listens in silence but hears nothing.

James: So let's go see who's down there. Smack the twat in the gob then. The fuckin' perve.

Candy: Don't be fucking stupid. There's something wrong in here. It wasn't normal.

James: Wasn't normal? What the fuck do you think you saw then? You think you saw a ghost or something? (*Mocks her with exaggerated ghostly sounds*).

Candy: (*Pauses for a moment and replies in a terrified tone*) Shut up.
Stop. Stop it now. Yes!

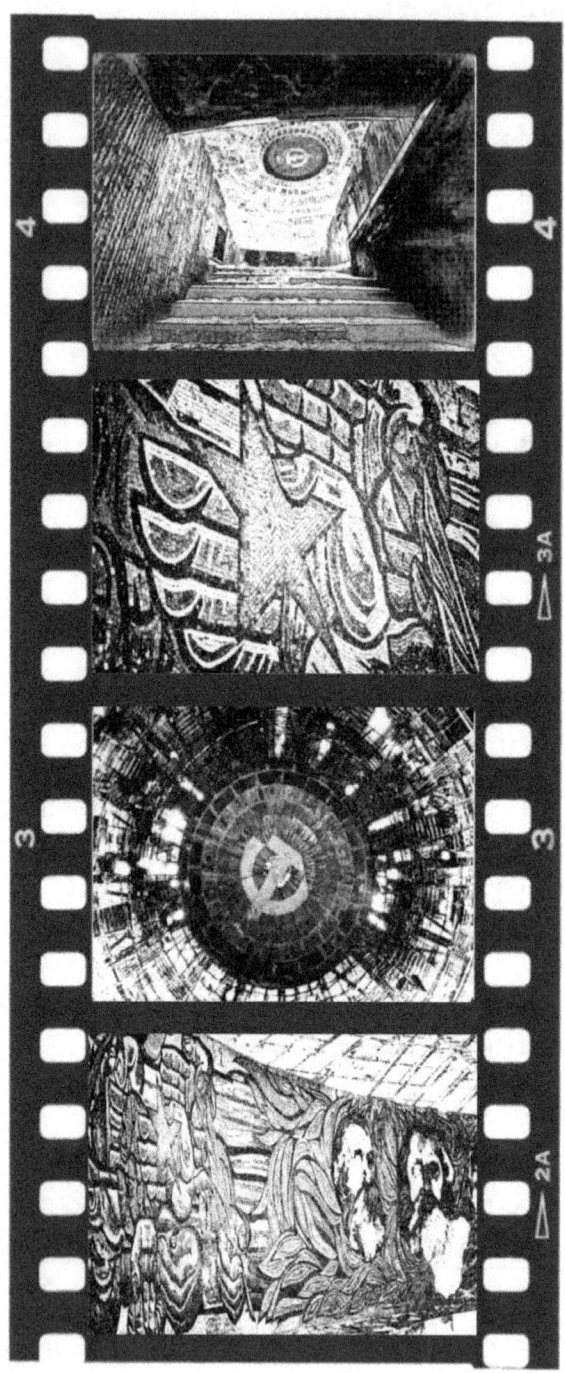

28

SCENE SEVEN: Dome

Kate is examining and cataloguing artwork around the inner walls of the dome. She reads into her Dictaphone. Poor quality audio is picked up and duplicated by her helmet camera.

Kate: So here we are, inside the former Communist House at Shipka Peak in Bulgaria. Welcome all of you to Buzludzha. James and Candy are in the basements below. Alex and Jade have gone up the tower and Gunner - well he's gone solo looking for a tunnel that apparently may or may not exist, and that may or may not lead to a subterranean laboratory. But for now, this is me speaking, so for all of you folks watching this at home - Hi, I'm Kate. I want to start by explaining the purpose of the project for which we thank you. Oh yes we do! Without you guys watching this, and the generous funding you have provided, well, needless to say, there would be no project at all, so again, and firstly, thank you! So here it is: Soviet Ghosts. This project is part of our media submission for our masters. We're here today to talk about iconic socialist era constructions, architecture and brutalist structures you either love or hate. And where better to start than here. I'm sure you agree. Buzludzha was built in... (*Lightning strikes roof and interrupts her mid speech*)

Kate: (*Now continues*) Fuck! What the fuck was that? Something just touched me. I felt it, it was like electricity running through me, and it just tried to pull me over.

Her head cam continues to film as she silently scans the room, but nothing can be seen.

Kate: Okay, that's the freakiest thing. I don't know what you will see on film but, I swear, something just touched me… not touched, more like grabbed at me. Okay, let me start again then. Buzludzha was built in…

Physically scared and shocked she attempts to continue as she composes herself.

Kate: (*Continues*) …was built, in fact opened in 1981, on the site of a battle between Bulgarian rebels led by Hadji Dimitar and Stefan Karadzha against the Ottoman yoke of Turkish occupation. It's 4,726 feet above sea level and takes its name from the Turkish word meaning icy peak. It was built by the former communist regime to commemorate the events of 1891, when Dimitar Blagoev met in secret with other agrarians on this site to form the first Bulgarian socialist party: The Bulgarian Social Democratic Party. As you can see it is now derelict and….

Scene fades out as Kate continues her commentary.

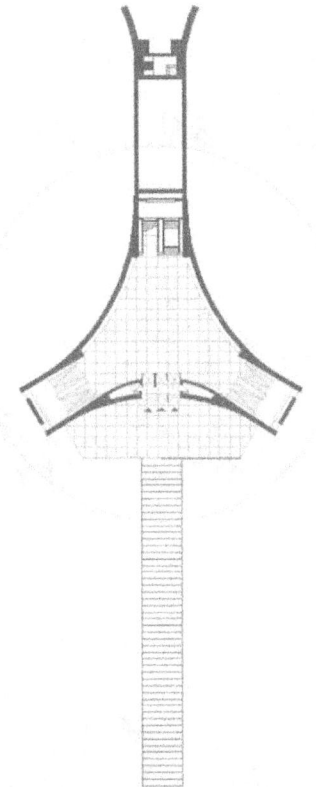

Spine

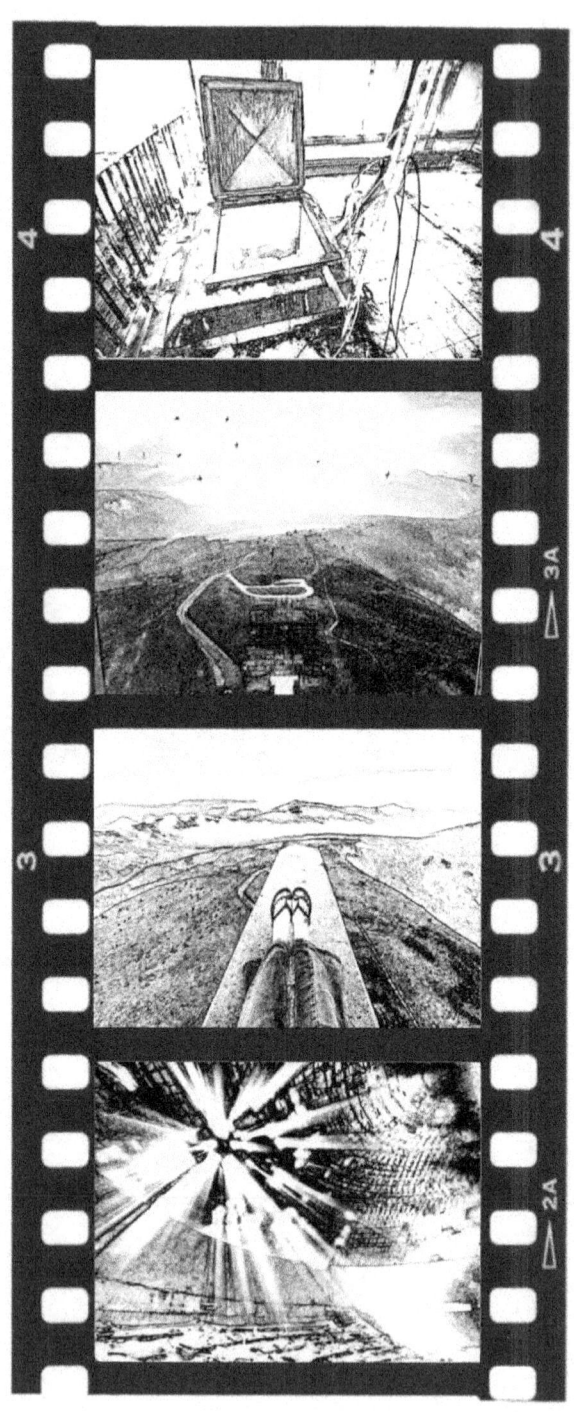

SCENE EIGHT: Lightening

Footage cuts back to Alex and Jade in the tower.

Alex: Okay, tripod's as solid as a rock now. I'm ready when you are Jade?

Jade: So here we are, up the tower. We wanted to go out onto the roof but as you can hear clearly, and no doubt you can catch the flashes too, there is a thunderstorm brewing, and yes, as you can also see, the ladders here are metal. So not a good idea. We'll try and catch that bit for you later on, in the morning. So, let me tell you about the star behind me and then we're gonna get the hell out of here. The star, the largest ever built in Russia was made out of... (*Lighting strikes and Alex is thrown violently from his feet*).

Jade: Alex, Alex, fuck Alex... talk to me. (*As no response is received, panicking, she now attempts mouth to mouth*). Don't die, fucking come on man, breath.

Alex: (*Coughs and draws in breathe deeply and suddenly. Mumbles*) What happened? Where am I?

Jade: Thank God. Can you hear me? Speak to me? Alex, say something.

Alex: (*A now terrified expression as he re-gains his senses*) Run Jade, run, get out, get out now.

Jade: What do you mean, run? Run from what? I'll go and get help.

Alex: Run! It's here. It's with us. I can see it. Run!

Jade: There's nothing here Alex. You're in shock. I'll go for help.

Alex: It's here. Run! (*Grasping Jade's wrist firmly, he reiterates*) Run. Go now. Leave me. Run. You have to run!

Jade: I'll be back. Hold on, I'll get you down from here. Just hold on. You're in shock.

Jade frantically descends from the tower in search of help. In her haste through the darkness she slips and falls. There's a loud crack as of bone breaking. Her leg is shattered.

Jade: (*Screaming in agony*) Jesus, Jesus, fuck, help. Fucking help me someone!

She senses a presence. Something or someone is descending the stairs above her. It is pure evil. She starts to crawl her way down, back toward the dome, finally losing strength beside the lift shaft of the first floor stairwell.

    Jade: (*Panting and crying, sniffling*) Help. Please help me, someone please. Please help me, I'm here. Alex, is that you? Alex?

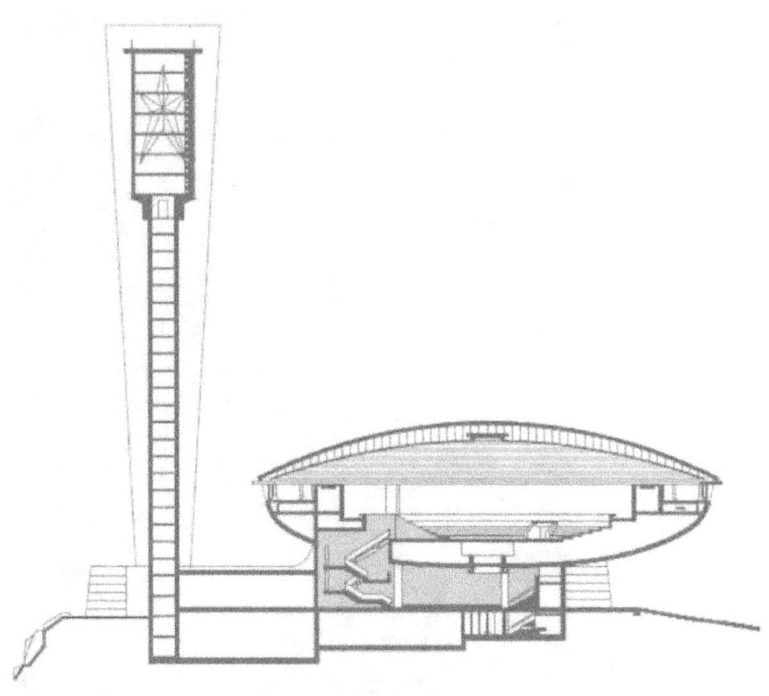

East View

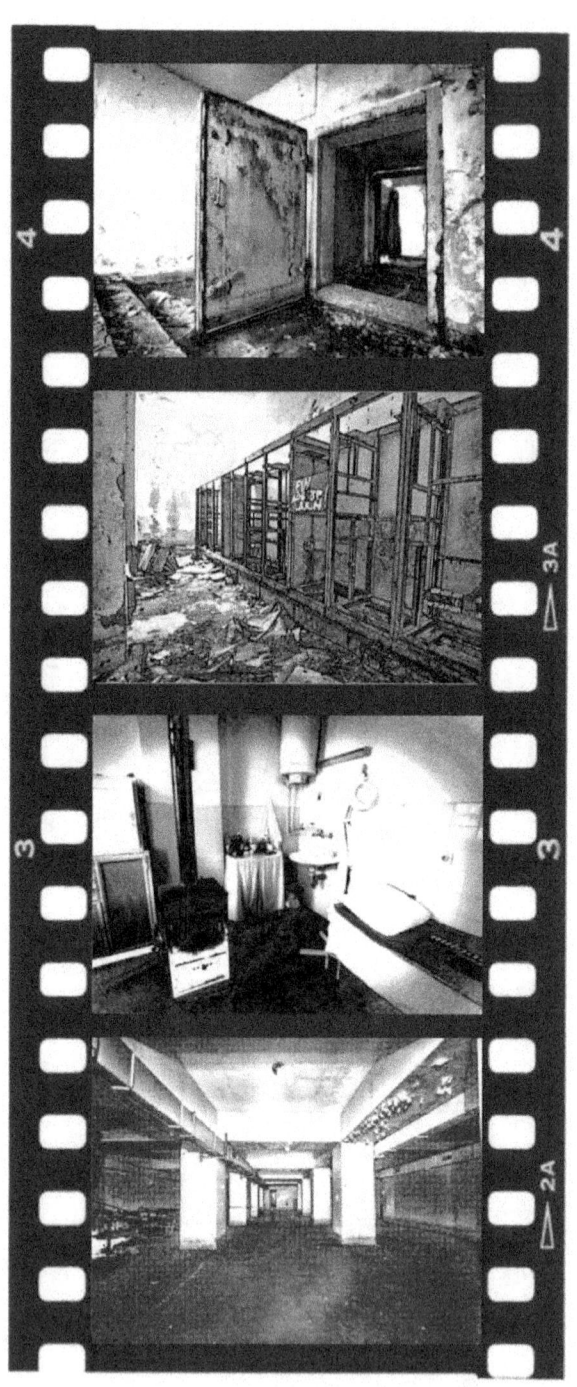

SCENE NINE: Tunnels

Gunner's head cam films as he struggles through a drainage pipe, at times using a rope to secure him from falls. The storm has brought heavy rainfall and risks washing him back down the pipe to certain death. He speaks into his camera.

Gunner: Well guys (*Jokingly*), the road to hell is pathed with good intentions and this seemed like a good idea at the time. There is some good news though; at least Kate had the sense to break away from it.

Gunner: (*Later continues*) So here's the situation. I found it, the way in down in the woods way below the building. It's difficult to crawl through but doable. Ropes are essential! I guess I'm kind of midway now. I feel like I've been climbing through for hours but (*Shows watch to the camera*) it's now 9.40. I guess there's one hell of a storm going on up there. The tunnel seems to be flooding. The decision is, do I turn back now and risk being washed away or carry on upward? The tunnels much thinner back down, or I guess, I'll carry on until I eventually level out into the basement. If it exists that is. I frigging hope so!

Gunner: (*Later continues after more progress*) So dudes, if you find this footage later washed up, I guess (*Jokingly, but clearly scared and saving face*) that means I'm dead. I'm still going on though, it's all here in the camera, but I can see a shaft ahead, I'm going on again. Catch you later!

He stares up a large vertical shaft with an iron access ladder. He starts to climb. He finds himself within a basement. Though clearly unused for some time, the basement is not as derelict as the remainder of the building. There is evidence of an old laboratory and he finds a room with what look like sick beds.

There are stairways to two upper tiers. He starts to read old documents from desk drawers but cannot understand them as some are written in some form of Hebrew and others in Bulgarian. However; horrific illustrations of human degradation and torture are all apparent. After some time here, he now hears noises behind him. Footsteps. It is the Russian.

Russian: Get out, get out! You cannot be here.

Gunner: Fuck man, you frightened the shit out of me.

Russian: Get out now!

Gunner: Are you here for the phone? You dropped it last night man. I didn't give it back because you were too drunk. I was going to give it back tomorrow at the hut, when I was back at the hostel... honest. I was just looking after it for you. I couldn't find you when I left, earlier on today but...

Russian: (*Interrupts Gunner*) Get out now. You cannot be here. Listen to me. Get out whilst you still can.

Gunner: I don't understand. Its derelict man. Nobody owns it. What the fuck's it got to do with you if I'm here or not?

Russian: It breathes. Life returns in the electricity. This building lives during the storms. Get out now! You must get out whilst you still can.

Lighting again strikes and the pair feel a surge of power within the fabric of the building around them. Suddenly an unknown force, an unseen entity starts pulling the Russian toward the tunnel entrance shaft. Gunner grabs at his wrists but is unable to counteract the enormous power. Eventually he lets go. The Russian is dragged, screaming, and away into the darkness. Footage then caught on Gunner's head cam is captured as he, the Russian, is apparently now thrown by the invisible force down into the vertical shaft. All that is left is the Russian's torch, still on, lying on the ground. Panic struck, Gunner ascends upward in sheer terror. Eventually he hears Kate, moaning and groaning in pain above him. He finds his way into the lift shaft but above him, the old seized lift, rusted in place for several years, prevents him from gaining access to her.

Gunner: Jade, Jade, is that you?

Jade: Gunner! Thank God. Help me, my leg is smashed, I can't move. There's something here.

Gunner: We've got to get out, we have to go now, but I'm stuck, I can't get past the lift. Where are the others?

Jade: We were up the tower. Alex was struck by lightning. He went strange, he said he could see things, bad things.

Gunner: Jade, don't worry. I'm gonna get you out, but I need to go back down first. I'll be a fast as I can. I'm coming to get you, just hold on.

Gunner terrified but methodically commences the tunnel descent back out toward the open. He does not discover any remains of the Russian. Jade remains still, but is breathing heavily. James and Candy, having finished their basement exploration early, now come across her.

Candy: What the fuck happened Jade? Jesus sister, are you alright?

James: We need to patch up that leg quick.

Candy: What the fuck was that?

James: What?

Candy: That. Listen...

The sound of electrostatic noises can be heard approaching from both the stairway above and basement stairs below. It is deeply disturbing.

Jade: Get me out of here please, I beg you. Please get me out, don't leave me here. It's evil.

James: Were not leaving anyone. Come on, we're all getting' out of here right now, but I warn you Jade; it's gonna hurt!

Candy and James lift Jade to her feet, where she hops in severe pain, supported by the shoulders of her friends, back toward the inner dome.

Candy: (*En route conversation takes place*) Have you seen any of the others, Jade?

Jade: Gunner's gone for help. He's in a tunnel that leads back outside. He was under the lift but, but Alex...

Candy: (*Interrupting*) What about Alex?

Jade: He's still up the tower. He's hurt too. It's bad. I was rushing to get help when I fell. He's been electrocuted. He's mumbling like a mad man.

James: Don't worry about that for now. Gunner and I can get him down later, but you're first, we need to get your leg fixed up.

The noise of electrostatic power grows louder as some form of entity approaches from both directions. The sound contains distorted contorted multiple voices, begging to be saved from purgatory, "Save us, save us, save us...purgatory, save us." They flee together to the sanctuary of the dome.

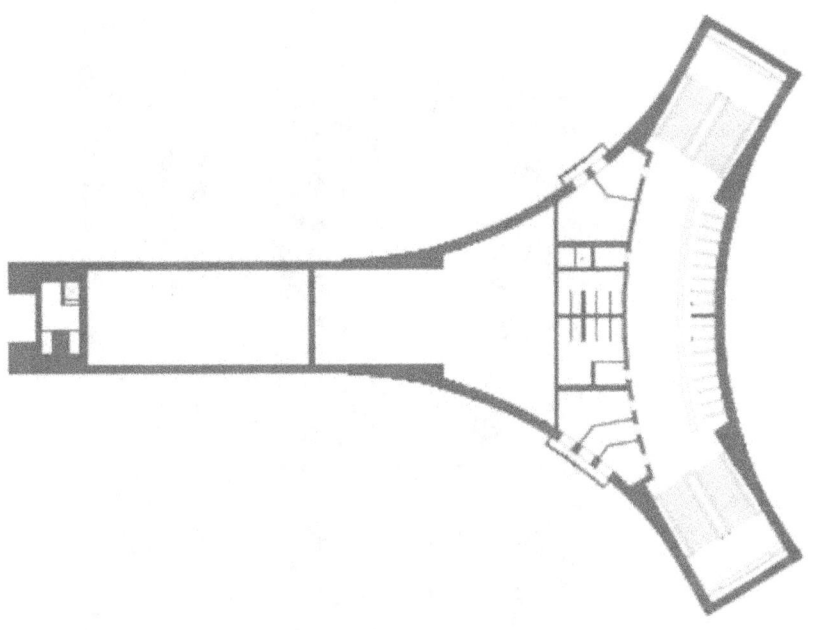

Stairway

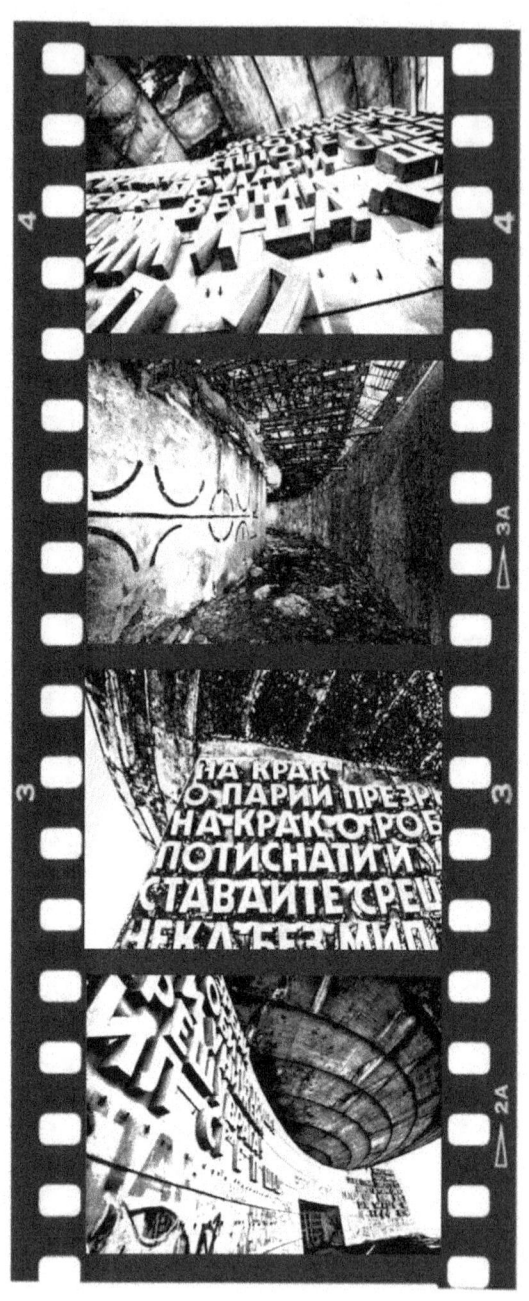

SCENE TEN: Sanctuary

42

James, Candy and Jade storm in to the inner domed area.

James: Quick, morphine Jade, we need the morphine, and bandages, now!

Kate: What the fuck happened?

Jade: It hurts Kate. Where's the morphine? I can't breathe properly.

James: Now! Where is it? Quickly. She's in agony.

Kate: Gunner took it. I don't have it. He went tunneling.

Jade: Fuck. He's gone back down now. He went for help.

James: I'll kill that fucking Kiwi arsehole. He'll fuckin pay for this one!

The group attempt to patch up Jade's leg the best they can under the circumstances. Lightning again strikes the building with enormous power; lighting up the entire dome ceiling above them. Beyond the broken roof and hammer and sickle central motif they look up to see Alex. He is stood on the apex of the tower above them.

Candy: What the fuck is he doing?

Kate: What the... Jesus Christ!

The group watch as Alex calmly steps off the tower without making a sound. He falls, crashing down onto the roof above them. His twisted mangled body hangs from a girder. His blood drips down making a pool at their feet. The building starts to throb. A pulsating energy force starts to light up the cylindrical walls around them, dimly on and off; in repeated electromagnetic pulses. Multiple figures appear to come from beyond the walls surrounding them, from within the concrete structure and slowly they approach the small group huddled in the middle of the room.

James: We need to get the fuck out now, let's go! Go!

Jade: Don't leave me, please, don't leave me.

Candy: Get up Jade, now, we need to run. Get up!

Kate: Fuck; what is it? What are they?

Struggling to hold up Jade and her body weight slowing them down whilst attempting to run up the stairs to the dome's outer balcony they all stumble to the ground together. Jade is pulled back down the steps toward the center by a mystery force. Alex's body now falls to the floor beside her. They both begin to spin in ever increasing circles with increasing speed within a gravity-free environment.

Jade: (*Screaming hysterically*) Help! God help me. I don't want to die, please, help me. Someone help me!

Now within the balcony area beyond the steps, James, Candy and Kate look on. Helpless to intervene as Jade and the remains of Alex's corpse are ripped apart organ by organ, limb by limb, by the ever increasing force. As they rotate, their body parts smash outward against the outer dome walls. And now they are both sucked into the wall; absorbed, disappearing without trace. Not a drop of blood is left afterward. What remains of the group now run in sheer terror and panic around the balcony in a desperate search for an exit. Breathless they stop.

Kate: There is no way out guys. We can run forever. We've just come back to where started.

Candy: There must be a way out... for Christ sake, there must be.

Kate: Believe me, there isn't. I wish there was, but there isn't.

James: The ropes? Where are the ropes? We can abseil down the outer walls, to the ground, look. (*He drops a stone over to prove his point*). It's not that far.

Kate: There are no ropes James. Gunner took mine with him and Jade's must still be up the tower.

Candy: You mean the only way out is back through the dome to the inner stairs? This is so fucked up.

James: We have to do something. We can't just run around in circles all night. My head torch is already starting to dim. I left my rucksack, with the spare kit downstairs.

Candy: Listen; Jade told us Gunner had gone for help, right? So we can wait for him. Someone will come, they must.

James: We don't even know if Gunner's still alive. Just look at the rain. If he's in a tunnel he might have been washed away now?

Candy: But we have to do something. I'm not going to end up like the others. I'm not, I'm not.

Kate: When I was alone earlier, waiting for the meet-up time, I felt something, it touched me. And it was there again every time the lighting struck. It was inexplicable so...

James: So what?

Kate: I found out online that this building used to house a hadron collider. The communists used it in experiments, to access a portal to outer worlds beyond outer space.

James: I've read that crap too. It's fiction. 'Communists in Outer Space', it's just cheap pulp fiction. It's bullshit Kate.

Candy: Does this look like fucking fiction to you prick. This is real shit and it's happening to us now. Right here, right now! And you need to get us the fuck out of here. Just fuckin' man up will you!

Kate: The book said that the collider was deactivated after the regime fell, but souls were trapped within the building's structure, in limbo, a purgatory from which they could not return. But they do, when the lighting strikes. It's true, all of it. They can come back.

James: Are you saying that the electricity brings them back to life? What the fuck are you on Kate?

Candy: What else is it? We all saw them come from within the walls. Kate, you saw them didn't you? Tell him it's true.

Kate: James, you saw exactly what just happened. Don't even try to deny it. That was some kind of electrical tornado and our friends are dead as a result. We don't need a cunt head here; you fucking saw it too.

James: So what now? We wait for the next surge or do we get the fuck out of here?

Kate: They can only exist momentarily when the lighting strikes. As the surge discharges, they disappear again. But, with each strike their power grows. It's storing electricity somehow. There must be batteries somewhere or something.

Candy: That's it Kate. We wait for the next strike, and then we leg it down to the exit below... out through the hole we came in by.

James: If we can make it to the hole bashed through the outer wall then... (*Kate interrupts him*).

Kate: James; I'm confused. I can't find my bearings. Which stairwell was the hole on?

   The group face each other in silence as not one of them can remember how to find the way out.

SCENE ELEVEN: **Headless**

Footage now cuts to Gunner. He has finally struggled down and is nearing the exit to the pipe. He is shivering with cold, the water almost drowning him as he struggles to catch his breathe. He can see moonlight at the outer end and continues determinedly on. On hands and knees he finally exits.

Gunner: Thank God, thank God... God I love you!

At that point, an axe is brought down onto the back of his neck. A single clean swipe removes it from his torso. With his head cam still recording as it remains strapped to his head, it is placed into his killer's woven sack.

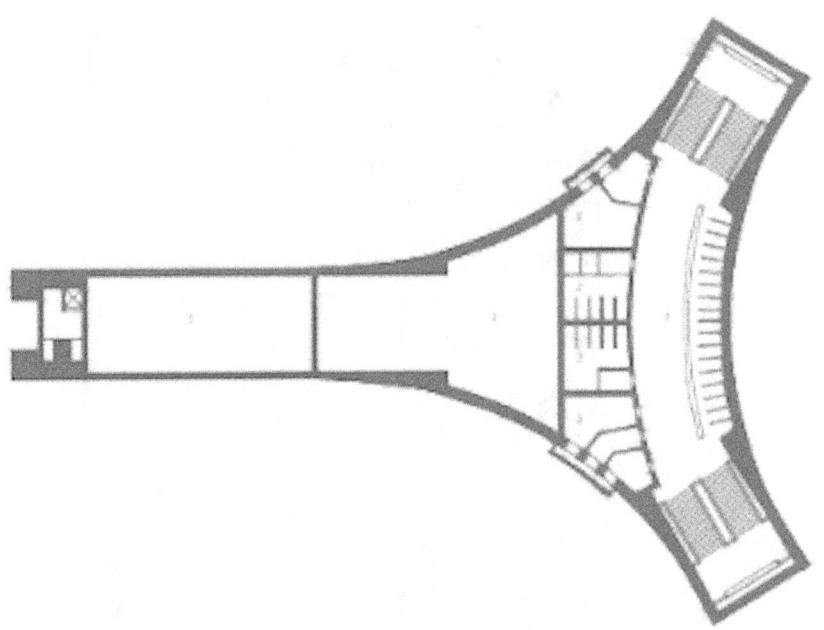

Underground

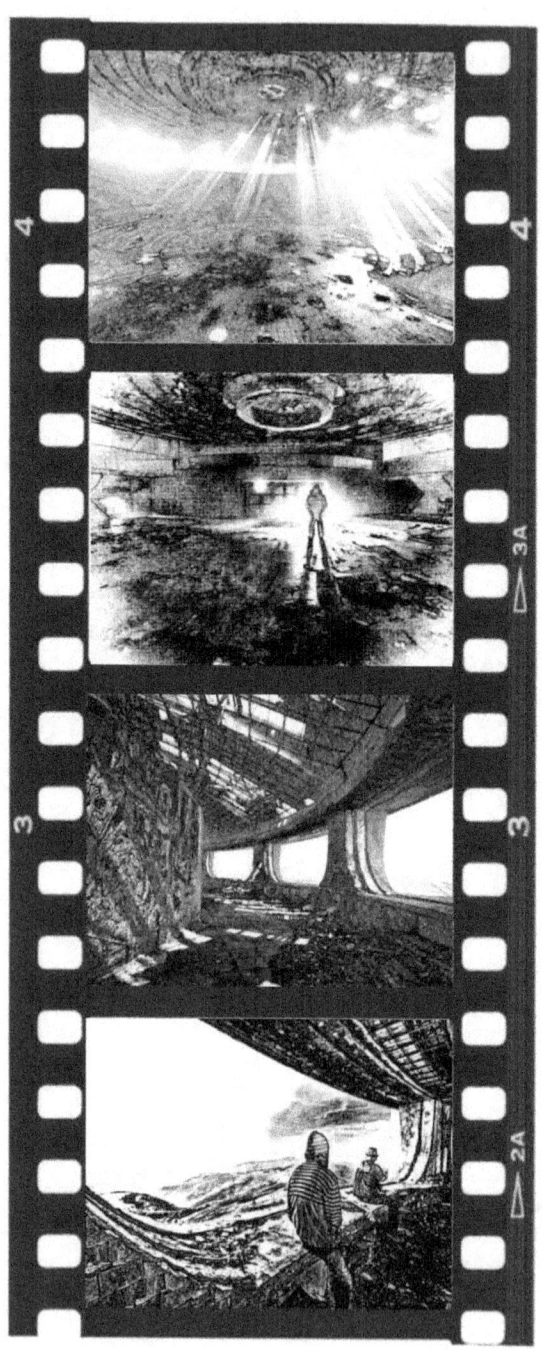

SCENE TWELVE: Hopelessness

Captured footage now shows us a return to the balcony where the group await the next surge. They look outward into the darkness and torrential rain.

James: Look; it's Gunner, he did it, there, I can see him. He's on the steps.

Kate: He's got the rope bag. Fucking way to go Gunner, fucking way to go.

Candy: That's not Gunner.

James: Gunner, Gunner, we're up here. (*Waving frantically*) Gunner!

Kate: (*Also waving*) Here Gunner. We're on the balcony above you!

Candy: Stop, I'm telling you, that's not Gunner!

They continue to peer down into the darkness as the figure slowly approaches them, climbing the pathed steps to the front of Buzludzha. It stops below them, looks up momentarily and then throws the sack up to them from below. It lands beside them.

Kate: Is it the ropes. Is it?

Shining their head torches upon it, they locate the blood soaked package. James lifts it slowly by both outer bottom corners. Gunner's head rolls out. Candy runs, screaming and terrified, back into the dome. James, her lover, follows.

James: Stop, Candy, stop, we must wait, stop, don't run.

Candy: I'm not dying in here, I'm not. It's not gonna happen to me, I'm not dying here.

She reaches the stairs but in her desperate flee for safety she falls down into the bottomless darknesS

of the stairwell below. Looters have removed the metal stairway balustrades. As she now falls, her neck is snapped. James peers down on her from considerable height above.

James: No, no, no, please, no, Candy, no. Oh, Jesus no.

Lightning strikes. James feels a presence behind him. He turns to see multiple silhouettes; black and featureless. They pull on him, and after falling over, he is now taken, dragged by his ankles into the walls. Just as a sponge expels water, the walls are sodden with flesh and blood. Eventually evaporating within, absorbing his remains as if nothing had happened at all. His head torch and camera, and all other metal non-porous objects remain on the floor below.

Kate: (*Screams out*) James, Candy, where are you, come back. James, Candy, don't leave me here. Come back, where are you?

(*Thunder has dulled the noise of their screams*)

Eventually; after many hopeless hours she now falls, shattered and exhausted, shivering, into a deep sleep, huddled under the overhanging concrete sill of the outer derelict window sockets.

Kate: (*Awakening and neurotically talking to herself*) I'm on the outer boundary of the building. They can't get me here, they can't. I know this, get a grip, just need to focus, pull myself together and wait for daylight. If, if... if I stay under here they cannot get me. They didn't get Alex did they? No, no... he jumped by himself to get away from them. Focus Kate, focus.

The storm subsides whilst she sleeps and daylight finally arrives. Still terrified but composed she stands. She finds that Gunner's head has disappeared, but his camera remains on the floor at her feet.

Kate: (*Continuing insanely to chant to herself*) They took it. It was absorbed. Yes, his head, they took, took it into the walls when I slept. The cameras. I need the cameras. I have to collect the cameras. They won't believe me. I need the cameras. I must find them all. Focus, I must find them.

She picks up Gunner's camera, and after entering the dome, locates Alex's and Jade's also. They are smashed from violent impact so she removes both memory cards. She also collects the group's additional memory cards and back-ups from personal baggage left behind at the scene. James's video camera is later found beside a stair well and Candy's is on the floor of the main hallway below the dome. She kneels, having emptied her own personal kit bag, as she now frantically packs everything else, her finds, back into her own backpack. She steadily begins to collect her own thoughts.

Now with the storm long over and bright daylight shining in through openings in the roof above, she finds her way back to the small exit hole. One large enough for just one person at a time to crawl through and out into the open air beyond. It was smashed through the outer wall and led out onto the first floor landing, the very same one through which the group had entered the previous day. After the main doorway gates to the complex had been previously welded shut, to prevent continued looting, this new borehole had been the only way for tourists and sightseers to gain entry. Dropping her rucksack outside to the floor first, she pulls her way through into the broad daylight beyond.

Kate: No! Dear God, no, please not me, no… I beg you, no… Please! Don't take me!

Kate realises that something or somebody has grabbed her by the ankles. Powerless, she is pulled back into the hole from which she came, feet first. Two of her finger nails are caught by her own head cam as they are ripped from her fingers. They fall to the bloodsplattered ground outside below her as she desperately attempts to cling to, and accordingly violently scratches the concrete surface of the outer walls.

Footage cuts to a source of unknown origin. Not video previously captured and recovered from the group's own head cams but a return to the film's opening sequence. That dark dank cellar in which a woman appears to be starved alongside an older man being stripped of his own flesh. A figure walks around to the front of the video cam.

Holding a blooded sack in his left hand which is obviously the remains of Gunner's head, the killer now removes his hood and reveals himself.

His face is that of the covert agent, Arat (the missing Vicar known as Jeremy Walton).

-End-

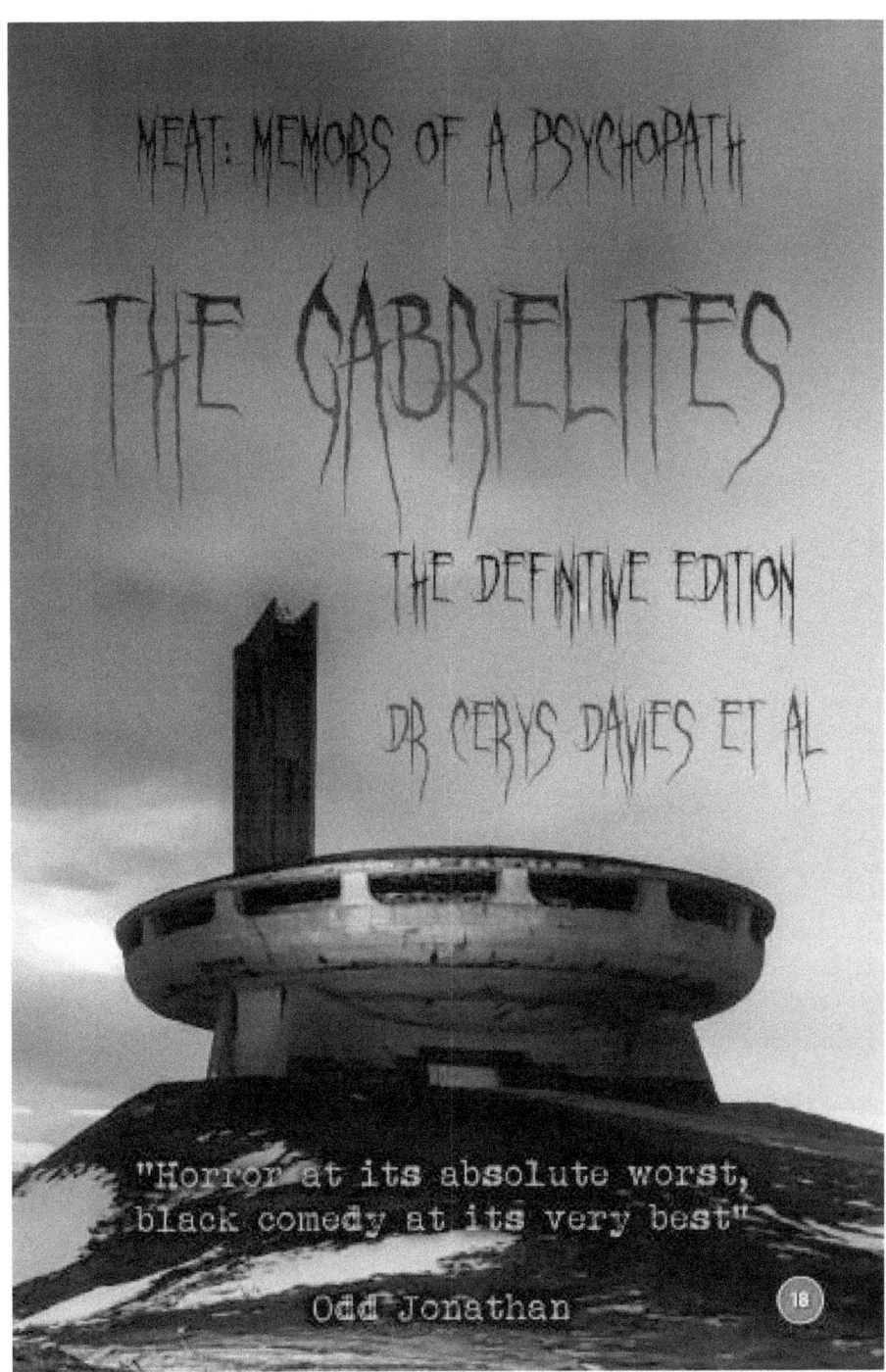

MEAT: MEMOIRS OF A PSYCHOPATH

THE GABRIELITES

THE DEFINITIVE EDITION

DR CERYS DAVIES ET AL

"Horror at its absolute worst,
black comedy at its very best"

Odd Jonathan

www.ingramcontent.com/pod-product-compliance
Lightning Source LLC
Chambersburg PA
CBHW072254170526
45158CB00003BA/1073